5169

Patterns

David Kirkby

First published in Great Britain by Heinemann Library
an imprint of Heinemann Publishers (Oxford) Ltd
Halley Court, Jordan Hill, Oxford OX2 8EJ

MADRID ATHENS PARIS
FLORENCE PRAGUE WARSAW
PORTSMOUTH NH CHICAGO SAO PAULO
SINGAPORE TOKYO MELBOURNE AUCKLAND
IBADAN GABERONE JOHANNESBURG

Designed by The Pinpoint Design Company
Printed in China

99 98 97 96 95
10 9 8 7 6 5 4 3 2 1

ISBN 0431 07956 0

British Library Cataloguing in Publication Data available on
request from the British Library.

Acknowledgements
The Publishers would like to thank the following
for the kind loan of equipment and materials
used in this book: Boswells, Oxford; The Early Learning
Centre; Lewis', Oxford; W. H. Smith; N. E. S. Arnold.
Special thanks to the children of St Francis C.E. First School

The Publishers would like to thank the following for
permission to reproduce photographs: J. Allan Cash Ltd. p 5;
Robert Harding Picture Library p 6.
All other photographs: Chris Honeywell, Oxford

Cover photograph: Chris Honeywell, Oxford

Contents

You can make patterns by using one or more shapes over and over. These all have patterns on them.

The black and white stripes on a zebra crossing make a pattern.

All these things have stripes.
Which things have stripes that
run across them?
Which things have stripes that
go up and down?

To do:
Make up your own
patterns with stripes.
Use a ruler to make
straight stripes.
Can you make a curved
stripe pattern?

Stripes make patterns. Spots make patterns too.

Some animals have stripes.

What makes the pattern on
a ladybird?

To do:
Copy the spot pattern
that makes 6.
Make some different
patterns with 6 spots.

Colours can make patterns.
The next fish will be blue.

These beads make a colour pattern.

What colour patterns can you see?

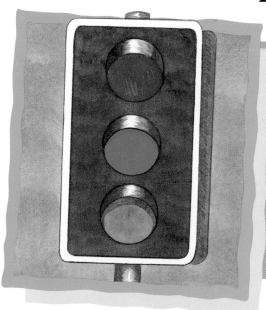

To do:
What pattern do traffic lights make as they change colour? Copy the fish on page 8. Make a pattern of your own with 8 fish. They do not have to be in a straight line.

A check pattern
has squares of
different colours.

This shirt has a
check pattern.

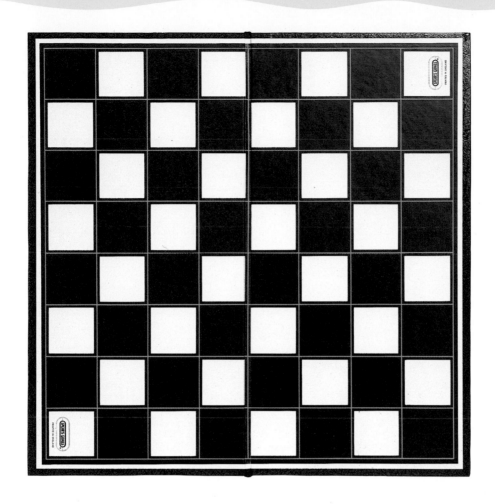

How many black squares are there?
How many white squares are there?

To do:
Design and colour
a check pattern
for a flag.

11

Solid shapes, like cylinders, can make patterns. We call these stacking patterns.

These boxes are stacked in rows. They go across the shelf.

These books are stacked
in columns.
The piles go up.

To do:
Stack some bricks of the
same size in rows.
Stack some bricks of the
same size in columns.
Can you stack the bricks
in any other patterns?

Squares tessellate.
The shapes fit
together with
no gaps.

These tiles tessellate.

This football has 2 different shapes.
Do they tessellate?

To do:
Trace around this
shape several times.
Cut out your shapes.
Arrange them to see
if they tessellate.

15

Pictures can make patterns. They do not tessellate.

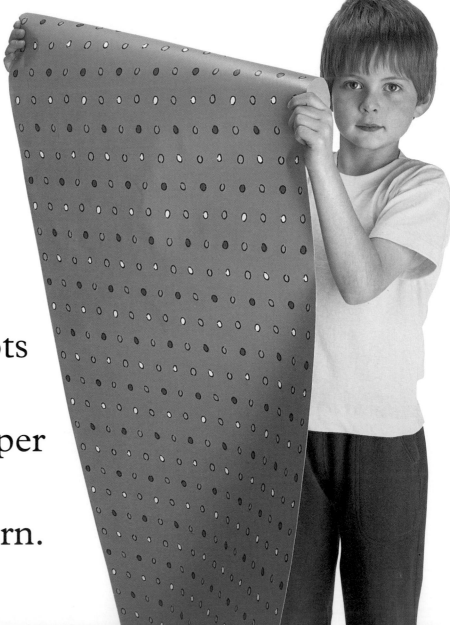

The dots on the wallpaper make a pattern.

16

Do the stars on the curtains
make a pattern?

To do:
Draw a rectangle.
Use a ruler.
Make a picture pattern
for a bedcover.

You can find
patterns anywhere.

These bricks make patterns.

What patterns can you see here?

To do:
Copy the jumper
pattern.
Design a jumper
pattern of your own.

The numbers on the houses in a street make a pattern.

The houses on this side of the road have odd numbers.
The next numbers will be 9 and 11.

The houses on this side have even numbers.

What will the next 2 numbers be?

To do:
Write down all the odd numbers from 1 to 20.
Write down all the even numbers from 1 to 20.

Symmetrical things have 2 matching halves.

The 2 matching halves can be anywhere.

Where can you cut this fruit
to make 2 matching halves?

To do:
Draw some things
you wear that are
symmetrical.

answers

Page 5   The cushion, T-shirt and cup have stripes going across.

The wash-bag and towel have stripes going up and down

Page 7   Spots

Page 9   Red, yellow, red, yellow

Page 11   32 black squares, 32 white squares

Page 15   Yes

Page 17   Yes

Page 19   Spots, checks, stripes, picture patterns, diamonds

Page 21   6, 8

Page 23   Anywhere that cuts through the centre

---

index